8|12

Welcome
to the World,

ZooBorns!

by Andrew Bleiman and Chris Eastland

The photos in this book were previously published in
ZooBorns: The Newest, Cutest Animals from the World's Zoos and Aquariums.

Ready-to-Read

Simon Spotlight

New York London Toronto Sydney New Delhi

SIMON SPOTLIGHT

An imprint of Simon & Schuster Children's Publishing Division

1230 Avenue of the Americas, New York, New York 10020

Text copyright © 2012 by ZooBorns LLC

Photos copyright © 2010 by ZooBorns LLC

The photos in this book were previously published in *ZooBorns: The Newest, Cutest Animals from the World's Zoos and Aquariums*. All rights reserved, including the right of reproduction in whole or in part in any form.

SIMON SPOTLIGHT, READY-TO-READ, and colophon are registered trademarks of Simon & Schuster, Inc.

For information about special discounts for bulk purchases, please contact Simon & Schuster Special Sales at 1-866-506-1949 or business@simonandschuster.com.

The Simon & Schuster Speakers Bureau can bring authors to your live event. For more information or to book an event contact the Simon & Schuster Speakers Bureau at 1-866-248-3049 or visit our website at www.simonspeakers.com.

Manufactured in the United States of America 0312 LAK

First Edition

10 9 8 7 6 5 4 3 2 1

Bleiman, Andrew.

Welcome to the World, ZooBorns! / by Andrew Bleiman and Chris Eastland.

p. cm. — (Zooborns)

Summary: "Give a warm welcome to the awww-some ZooBorns animal babies!Get to know the adorable ZooBorns in this Ready-to-Read storybook that's chock-full of cute and cuddly baby zoo animals. With a familiar refrain of "Welcome to the world!" on every page, this photographic collection of irresistible critters is ideal for emerging readers"— Provided by publisher.

ISBN 978-1-4424-4377-8 (pbk.)

ISBN 978-1-4424-4376-1 (hardcover)

ISBN 978-1-4424-4378-5 (ebook)

1. Zoo animals—Infancy—Juvenile literature. I. Eastland, Chris. II. Title.

QL77.5.B5393 2012

591.3'92073—dc23

2011045350

Welcome to the wonderful world of
ZooBorns!

The newborn animals featured in this book live
in zoos around the world. Get to know them through
adorable photos and fun facts written in language that
is just right for emerging readers. Your child might not
be able to pronounce all the animal species names yet,
but if you stay close by, you can help sound them out.

This book can also be used as a tool to begin a
conversation about endangered species. The more
we learn about animals in zoos, the more we can do
to protect animals in the wild. Please visit your
local accredited zoo or aquarium to learn more!

This is Amani the aardvark.
Amani has such big ears
and so many wrinkles!

Welcome to the world,
baby aardvark!

Here is a newborn clouded leopard.

This little kitten will grow into a big cat.

Look at his milk mustache!

Welcome to the world,
baby leopard!

Say hello to Lana and Lucy!
Lana and Lucy are twin
emperor tamarins.

Welcome to the world, baby tamarins!

One, two, three
baby meerkats
are hiding in a burrow.
Soon they will come out to
explore.

Welcome to the world,
baby meerkats!

Splish, splash!

Kit the sea otter is a great
swimmer.

Kit swims with a shell in
her paws.

Welcome to the world,
baby sea otter!

Meet Kali and Durga.
They are brother and sister
Bengal tigers.
They have blue eyes
and white fur.

Welcome to the world,
baby tigers!

Mali the elephant loves to smile!

She also loves to have fun.

Her trunk will grow to be long and strong.

Welcome to the world,
baby elephant!

One fact about
Oliver the koala
is that he is not a bear!
Another fact about Oliver
is that he loves his mommy!

Welcome to the world,
baby koala!

Kai the spotted hyena
likes to sleep
with his legs in the air.
That is so silly!

Welcome to the world,
baby hyena!

These baby mongooses
rest all together
in a big, furry heap!
Welcome to the world,
baby mongooses!

Special thanks to the photographers and institutions that made ZooBorns! possible:

AARDVARK
Amani
Mark M. Gaskill, Phoenix Innovate,
taken at the Detroit Zoo

TIGERS
Kali and Durga
Robert La Follette, taken at Tampa's Lowry Park

TAMARINS
Lana and Lucy
Dave Parsons/Denver Zoo

ELEPHANT
Mali
Trent Browning/Melbourne Zoo

MEERKATS
Zoo Basel

CLOUDED LEOPARD
Smithsonian National Zoological Park

KOALA
Oliver
Richard Rokes/Riverbanks Zoo and Garden

SEA OTTER
Kit
Randy Wilder/© Monterey Bay Aquarium

HYENA
Kai
Dave Parsons/Denver Zoo

BANDED MONGOOSES
Cheryl Piropato/Fort Wayne Children's Zoo